My World of Geography
ISLANDS

Angela Royston

Heinemann
LIBRARY

young Explorer

www.heinemann.co.uk/library
Visit our website to find out more information about **Heinemann Library** books.

To order:
☎ Phone 44 (0) 1865 888066
▤ Send a fax to 44 (0) 1865 314091
▣ Visit the Heinemann Bookshop at www.heinemann.co.uk/library to browse our catalogue and order online.

First published in Great Britain by Heinemann Library, Halley Court, Jordan Hill, Oxford OX2 8EJ, part of Harcourt Education.
Heinemann is a registered trademark of Harcourt Education Ltd.

Editorial: Andrew Farrow and Dan Nunn
Design: Ron Kamen and Celia Jones
Illustrations: Jo Brooker (p. 13), Jeff Edwards (pp. 28–9)
Picture Research: Rebecca Sodergren, Melissa Allison and Debra Weatherley
Production: Duncan Gilbert

The paper used to print this book comes from sustainable resources.

ISBN 0 431 11800 0 (hardback)
ISBN 978 0 431 11800 0 (hardback)
08 07 06 05 04
10 9 8 7 6 5 4 3 2 1

ISBN 0 431 11805 1 (paperback)
ISBN 978 0 431 11805 5 (paperback)
09 08 07 06
10 9 8 7 6 5 4 3 2

British Library Cataloguing in Publication Data

Royston, Angela
Islands. – (My world of geography)
1. Islands – Juvenile literature
I. Title
551.4'2

A full catalogue record for this book is available from the British Library.

Acknowledgements

The Publishers would like to thank the following for permission to reproduce photographs:

Alamy Images pp. **15** (Dave Marsden), **16** (Robert Harding World Imagery), **20** (Adrian Muttitt), **21** (Jon Arnold Images), **24** (Nick Hanna); Corbis pp. **7** (Jon Sparks), **12** (Bob Krist), **17, 18, 25, 27**; Digital Vision p. **8**; Ecoscene p. **6** (John Farmer); FLPA p. **9** (S. Johnson); Getty Images/Image Bank p. **4**; Getty Images/Photodisc pp. **14, 26**; Harcourt Education Ltd p. **5**; Lonely Planet p. **22** (Wayne Walton); Natural History Photo Library p. **23**; Robert Harding Picture Library p. **19**; Science Photo Library p. **10**; Still Pictures p. **11**

Cover photograph reproduced with permission of Corbis/BSPI.

Every effort has been made to contact copyright holders of any material reproduced in this book. Any omissions will be rectified in subsequent printings if notice is given to the Publishers.

Contents

Some words are shown in bold, **like this**. You can find out what they mean by looking in the Glossary.

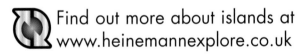

Find out more about islands at
www.heinemannexplore.co.uk

What is an island?

An island is a piece of land that is surrounded by water. Sometimes there are islands in lakes and rivers, but most islands are in the sea.

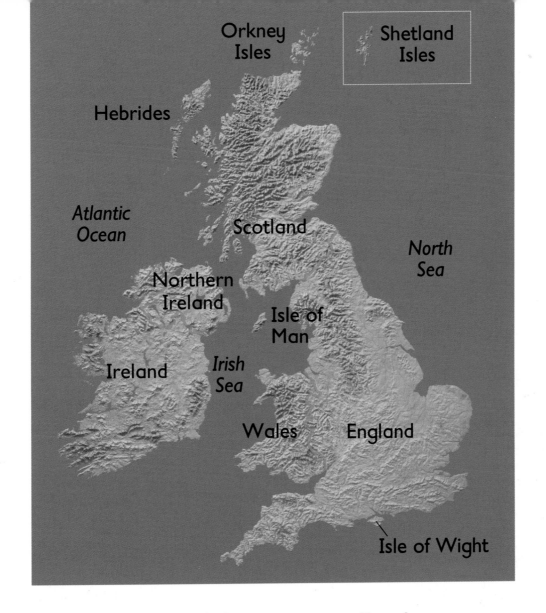

Islands can be big or small. This map shows the British Isles. The British Isles are made up of two big islands and many smaller islands.

Pieces of mainland

Some islands are pieces of **mainland** that have been cut off by the sea or a river. The water wore away the land between the island and the mainland.

This island used to be part of the mainland. The sea wore away the rocks between the island and the mainland.

Sometimes the level of the sea rises.
Seawater then covers large areas of
low land. What used to be the top of
a hill or mountain becomes an island.

Oceanic islands

Some islands are the tops of high mountains or **volcanoes** that rise up from the bottom of the sea. They are called **oceanic islands**.

This photo shows part of the coast of Hawaii Island, in the Pacific Ocean. The rocks are made of black lava from the volcano that formed the island.

The island of Surtsey rose out of the sea in 1963.

Surtsey is a **volcanic** island that rose up near the **coast** of Iceland. Some volcanic islands are still **erupting**. Others stopped erupting long ago.

Coral islands

Coral islands are made by millions of tiny sea animals called coral **polyps**. Coral polyps live in warm, shallow seas.

When a coral polyp dies, its **skeleton** remains. New coral polyps live on top of the skeletons. Over hundreds of years, the coral builds up to form an island.

Florida Keys

The Florida Keys are a line of small **coral** islands. The word 'Key' means 'small island'. Some of the islands are joined together by road bridges.

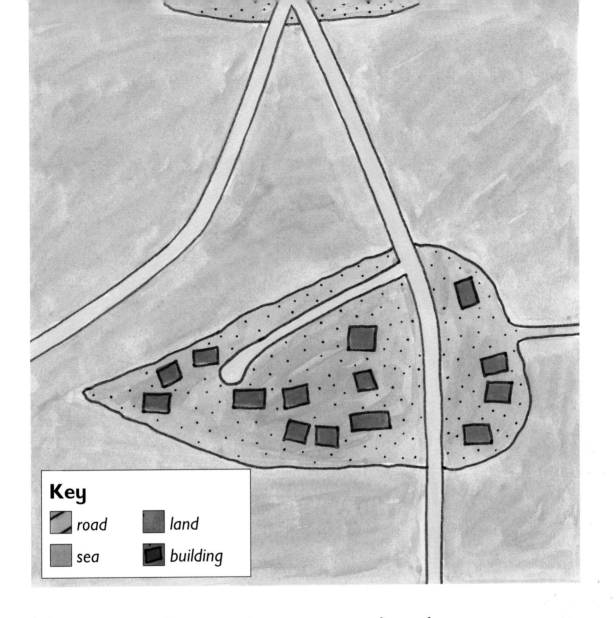

Key

◩ road   ■ land

■ sea   ■ building

This map shows the same island as the photo on page 12. It also shows the road that joins one island to the next. You could draw a map like this.

Wildlife

The plants and animals on most islands are the same as those on the nearby **mainland**. Islands without many people may become safe places for seabirds and other animals.

The animals on this island beach are elephant seals.

Some islands have plants and animals that are different from anywhere else in the world. **Tuataras**, like this, live only in New Zealand.

Farming and fishing

People who live on islands often get some of their food from farming. They grow **crops** and keep animals, such as sheep and goats.

Islands are surrounded by water, so
islanders can get food from fishing.
Some islanders earn money by
working for **tourists**.

Island cities

Some cities are built on islands. Many people live on the small island of Hong Kong. The buildings are made very tall to fit in more people.

Some cities began on an island but spread on to the **mainland**. Manhattan is an island in the Hudson River. It is also the centre of New York City!

Travelling to islands

You have to travel by boat or **hydrofoil** to reach most islands. Ships carry people, cars and things like food and clothes. Hydrofoils carry people.

Often, the quickest way to reach an island is by aeroplane. Planes carry **tourists** to and from islands where there is an airport.

Stopovers

Islands are useful places to stop during long journeys across the ocean. Ships stock up with fresh water and food before they continue their journey.

Island ports, like this one in the Azores, have been used by ships for hundreds of years.

This spotted flycatcher has stopped for a rest on the Mediterranean island of Minorca.

Some birds make long journeys, flying across seas and oceans. They may stop on an island for a short time to rest and wait for good weather.

Enjoying islands

People often like to go to an island for a holiday, particularly when the weather there is hot. **Tourists** enjoy spending time on the beach and swimming in the sea.

Easter Island in the Pacific Ocean is hard to get to. Tourists visit the island so they can see these huge stone statues.

All islands are different. Tourists can travel around an island to see the different plants and animals. They might also visit famous buildings or other attractions.

Spoiling islands

Some islands are being spoiled by people. Large hotels and airports are built for the **tourists**. Sometimes these buildings destroy beautiful parts of the island.

People visit **tropical** islands to see the **coral reefs**. But reefs are easily damaged by boats and divers who break off pieces of **coral**.

Islands of the world

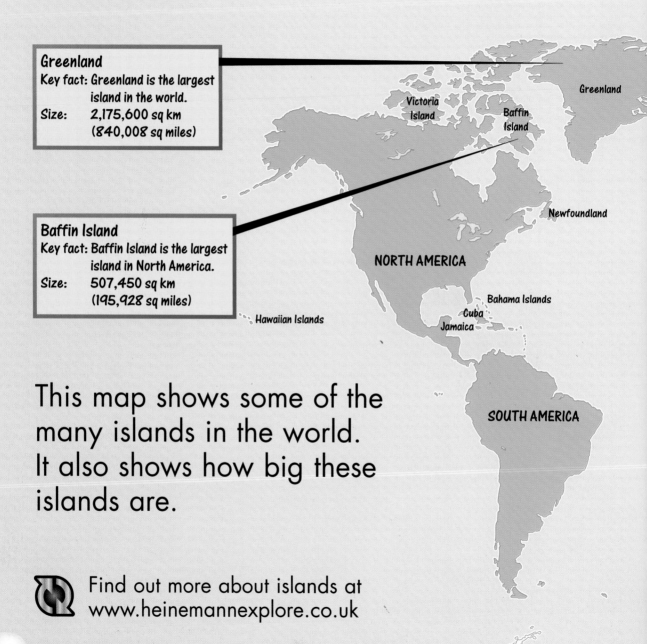

Greenland
Key fact: Greenland is the largest
island in the world.
Size: 2,175,600 sq km
(840,008 sq miles)

Baffin Island
Key fact: Baffin Island is the largest
island in North America.
Size: 507,450 sq km
(195,928 sq miles)

Greenland

Victoria
Island

Baffin
Island

Newfoundland

NORTH AMERICA

Bahama Islands

Cuba

Hawaiian Islands

Jamaica

SOUTH AMERICA

This map shows some of the
many islands in the world.
It also shows how big these
islands are.

Find out more about islands at
www.heinemannexplore.co.uk

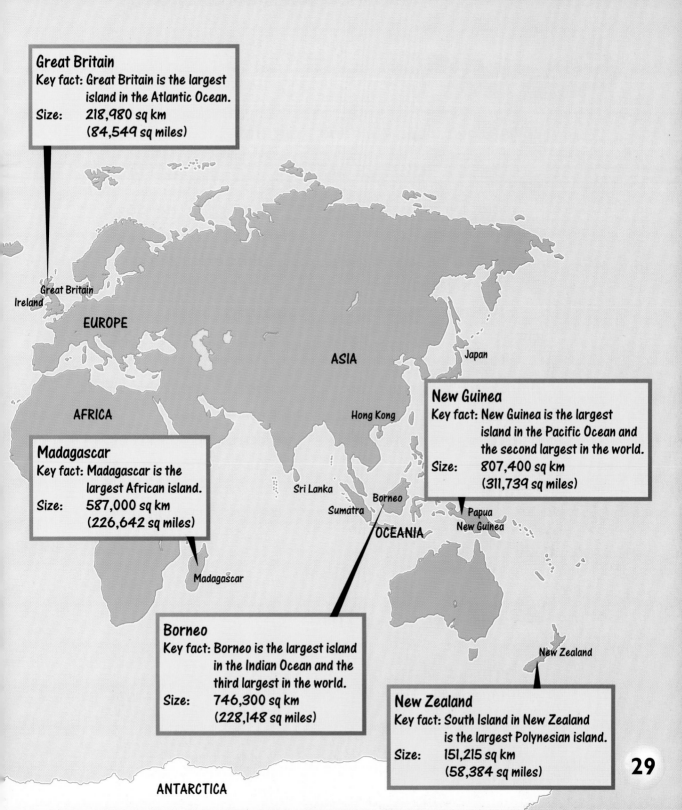

Great Britain
Key fact: Great Britain is the largest
island in the Atlantic Ocean.
Size: 218,980 sq km
(84,549 sq miles)

Madagascar
Key fact: Madagascar is the
largest African island.
Size: 587,000 sq km
(226,642 sq miles)

Borneo
Key fact: Borneo is the largest island
in the Indian Ocean and the
third largest in the world.
Size: 746,300 sq km
(228,148 sq miles)

New Guinea
Key fact: New Guinea is the largest
island in the Pacific Ocean and
the second largest in the world.
Size: 807,400 sq km
(311,739 sq miles)

New Zealand
Key fact: South Island in New Zealand
is the largest Polynesian island.
Size: 151,215 sq km
(58,384 sq miles)

Great Britain
Ireland
EUROPE
AFRICA
ASIA
Japan
Hong Kong
Sri Lanka
Sumatra
Borneo
OCEANIA
Papua
New Guinea
Madagascar
New Zealand
ANTARCTICA

29

Glossary

coast land along the edge of the sea

coral hard substance made from the skeletons of tiny animals

coral reef ledge of coral just underneath the surface of the sea

crops plants that farmers grow in their fields

erupting exploding or bursting out

hydrofoil boat that skims over the water

islanders people who live on an island

mainland large area of land that often forms a continent

oceanic island island far out in the ocean

polyp kind of tiny animal, found in the sea

skeleton animal's bones or shell

tourists people who visit a place on holiday

tropical coming from places that are on or near the Equator

tuatara type of lizard that only lives in New Zealand

volcanic made by a volcano

volcano mountain or crack in the ground through which hot, liquid rock from deep inside the Earth bursts out

Find out more

Further reading

Geography First: Islands by Chris Durbin (Hodder Wayland, 2004)

Info Trail: Would You Like To Live On a Small Island? (Longman, 2001)

Atlas One (Longman, 1994)

Make It Work! Geography: Maps by Andrew Haslam (Two-Can, 2000)

Geography Starts Here: Maps and Symbols by Angela Royston (Hodder Wayland, 2001)

Useful Websites

www.pitara.com/discover/geography/index.asp – use this website to compare islands such as Madagascar, Hong Kong and Greenland with the UK, USA or Australia.

Disclaimer

All the Internet addresses (URLs) given in this book were valid at the time of going to press. However, due to the dynamic nature of the Internet, some addresses may have changed, or sites may have changed or ceased to exist since publication. While the author and the Publishers regret any inconvenience this may cause readers, no responsibility for any such changes can be accepted by either the author or the Publishers.

Index